أعوذ بالله من الشيطان الرجيم

بسم الله الرحمن الرحيم

﴿الْحَمْدُ لِلَّهِ رَبِّ الْعَالَمِينَ ۝١ الرَّحْمَنِ الرَّحِيمِ ۝٢ مَالِكِ يَوْمِ الدِّينِ ۝٣ إِيَّاكَ نَعْبُدُ وَإِيَّاكَ نَسْتَعِينُ ۝٤ اهْدِنَا الصِّرَاطَ الْمُسْتَقِيمَ ۝٥ صِرَاطَ الَّذِينَ أَنْعَمْتَ عَلَيْهِمْ ۝٦ غَيْرِ الْمَغْضُوبِ عَلَيْهِمْ وَلَا الضَّالِّينَ ۝٧﴾

بسم الله الرحمن الرحيم

﴿قُلْ هُوَ اللَّهُ أَحَدٌ ۝١ اللَّهُ الصَّمَدُ ۝٢ لَمْ يَلِدْ وَلَمْ يُولَدْ ۝٣ وَلَمْ يَكُنْ لَهُ كُفُوًا أَحَدٌ ۝٤﴾

بسم الله الرحمن الرحيم

﴿قُلْ أَعُوذُ بِرَبِّ الْفَلَقِ ۝١ مِن شَرِّ مَا خَلَقَ ۝٢ وَمِن شَرِّ غَاسِقٍ إِذَا وَقَبَ ۝٣ وَمِن شَرِّ النَّفَّاثَاتِ فِي الْعُقَدِ ۝٤ وَمِن شَرِّ حَاسِدٍ إِذَا حَسَدَ ۝٥﴾

بسم الله الرحمن الرحيم

﴿قُلْ أَعُوذُ بِرَبِّ النَّاسِ ۝١ مَلِكِ النَّاسِ ۝٢ إِلَهِ النَّاسِ ۝٣ مِن شَرِّ الْوَسْوَاسِ الْخَنَّاسِ ۝٤ الَّذِي يُوَسْوِسُ فِي صُدُورِ النَّاسِ ۝٥ مِنَ الْجِنَّةِ وَالنَّاسِ ۝٦﴾

ما يَجِبُ عَلى المُسْلِمِ مَعْرِفَتُهُ
What is obligatory upon a Muslim to know

مَنْ رَبُّكَ؟
Who is your Lord?

رَبِيَ الله عز وجل
Allah is my Lord

مَا دِينُكَ؟
What is your Religion?

دِينِي الإِسْلامُ
My religion is Islam

مَنْ نَبِيُّكَ؟
Who is your prophet?

نَبِيِّ مُحَمَّدٌ ﷺ
My Prophet is Muhammad

اللّٰه ربّي

Allah is my lord

الإسلام ديني

Islām is my religion

محمد ﷺ نبيي

Muhammad sallallahualayhi wa salam is my prophet

ربي الله عز وجل

ديني الإسلام

نبي محمد صلى الله عليه وسلم

My Lord is Allah,(Glory be to him)
My religion is Al-Islam
My Prophet is Muhammad

أُجِيبُ بِالْكِتَابَةِ عَلَى الْحُرُوفِ الْمَنَقَّطَةِ

I trace the letters

مَنْ رَبُّكَ؟ ربي الله عز وجل.

مَا دِينُكَ؟ ديني الإسلام

مَنْ نَبِيُّكَ؟ نبي محمد صلى الله عليه وسلم.

Who is your Lord? Allah is my Lord

What is your Religion? My religion is Islam

Who is your prophet? My Prophet is Muhammad

Who is your Lord ?	دِيني الإسْلامُ
	مَنْ رَبُّكَ ؟
My religion is Al-Islam	
What is your religion ?	نَبِيي مُحَمَّدٌ
	مَا دِينُكَ ؟
My Prophet is Muhammad	
Who is your Propeht ?	رَبِّيَ الله عز وجل
	مَنْ نَبِيُّكَ ؟
My Lord is Allah Glory be to him	

أُرَتِّبُ الْكَلِمَاتِ الْآتِيَةَ

I order the following words

ربي الله	ربك؟	من	عز وجل
دينـي	مـا	دينك؟	الإسلام
مـن	نبيك؟	نبيـي	محمد

Glory be to him	Who	is you Lord?	My Lord is Allah
is Al-Islam	My religion	is your religion?	What
is Muhammad	is your prophet?	My Prophet	Who

٥

الله خالق كل شيء
Allah is the creator of everything

مَنْ خلقني؟ Who created me?

الله. Allah.

مَنْ خلق الناس؟
Who created the people?

الله. Allah.

مَنْ خلق السماوات والأرض والشمس والقمر؟
Who created the heavens, earth, sun and moon?

الله. Allah.

مَنْ خلق الحيوانات والطيور؟
Who created the animals and the birds?

الله. Allah.

مَنْ خَلَقَني ؟ اللّه

مَنْ خَلَقَ النَّاسَ ؟ اللّه

مَنْ خَلَقَ السَّماواتِ والأَرْضَ والشَّمْسَ والقَمَرَ ؟ اللّه

مَنْ خَلَقَ الحَيَواناتِ والطُّيورَ ؟ اللّه

Who created me? Allah
Who created the people? Allah
Who created the heavens , the earth,
the sun and the moon? Allah
Who created the animals and the birds? Allah

من خلقني؟ الله – من خلق الناس؟ الله

من خلق السماوات والأرض والشمس والقمر؟ الله

من خلق الحيوانات والطيور؟ الله

Who created me? Allah
Who created the people? Allah
Who created the heavens, earth, sun and moon? Allah
Who created the animals and birds? Allah

أُجِيبُ بِالْكِتَابَةِ عَلَى الْحُرُوفِ الْمُنَقَّطَة

I trace the letters

من خلقني؟ الله

من خلق الناس؟ الله

من خلق السماوات والأرض والشمس والقمر؟ الله

من خلق الحيوانات والطيور؟ الله

Who created me? Allah
Who created the people? Allah
Who created the heavens, earth, sun and moon? Allah
Who created the animals and birds? Allah

أَصِلُ الْكَلِمَةَ بِالْمَعْنَى الصَّحِيحِ
I join the word with the correct meaning

Allah	لِأَنَّنِي مُسْلِم	اللّٰه
Because I am Muslim		
Created me	إلا اللّٰه	خلقني
Except Allah		
There is no creator	اللّٰه	لا خالق
Allah is		
I obey Allah, the one who created me	خالق كل شيء	أطيع اللّٰه الذي خلقني
the creator of everything		

أُرَتِّبُ الْكَلِمَاتِ الْآتِيَةَ
I order the following words

اللّٰه ⬜	شيء ⬜	كل ⬜	خالق ⬜

⬜ Is the creator of	⬜ EveryThing	⬜ Allah

9

اللهُ يَرْزُقُنِي

Allah provides for me

اللهُ يَرْزُقُنِي ويَرْزُقُ جميع المخلوقات

**Allah provides for me
and All of creation**

اللهُ يَرْزُقُ النَّاسَ

**Allah provides for
the people**

اللهُ يَرْزُقُ الْحَيَوَانَ والطَّيْرَ

**Allah provides for
the animals and birds**

أَقْرَأُ وَأُلَوِّنُ
I read and colour

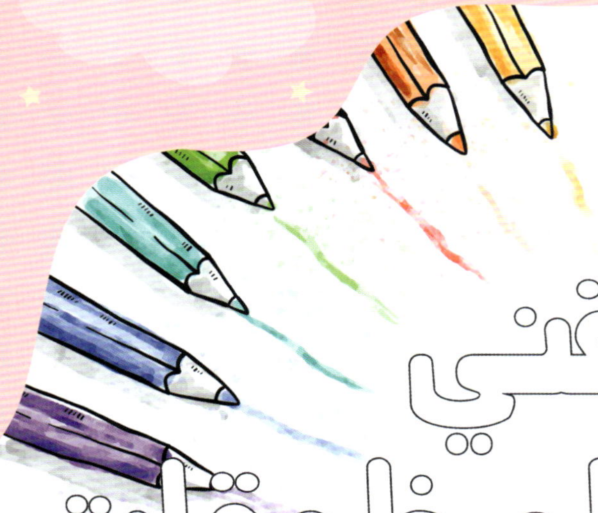

اللّه يرزقني
ويرزق جميع المخلوقات
اللّه يرزق الناس
اللّه يرزق الحيوان والطير

Allah provides for
the animals and birds
Allah provides for the people
Allah provides for me and the
rest of creation
Allah provides for me

الله يرزقني ويرزق جميع المخلوقات

الله يرزقني ـ الله يرزق الناس

الله يرزق الحيوان والطير

Allah provides for me and the rest of creation
Allah provides for me
Allah provides for the animals and birds
Allah provides for the people

أُجِيبُ بِالْكِتَابةِ عَلَى الْحُرُوفِ الْمُنَقَّطةِ

I trace the letters

من يرزقني ويرزق جميع المخلوقات؟ الله

من يرزقني؟ الله

من يرزق الحيوان والطير؟ الله

من يرزق الناس؟ الله

Who provides for me and the rest of creation? Allah
Who provides for me? Allah
Who provides for the animals and birds? Allah
Who provides for the people? Allah

أَصِلُ الْكَلِمَةَ بِالْمَعْنَى الصَّحِيحِ
I join the word with the correct meaning

| Allah | is Allah | هو الله | الله |

| The provider | Leave to search for its food | تسعى في البحث عن طعامها | الرزاق |

| The creation | Provides for me and the rest of creation | يرزقني ويرزق جميع المخلوقات | المخلوقات |

أُرَتِّبُ الْكَلِمَاتِ الْآتِيَةَ
I order the following words

| يرزق | الحيوان | والطير | الله |

| يرزقني | جميع | المخلوقات | ويرزق | الله |

| and birds | Provides for | The animals | Allah |

| provides for me | all of | The creation | He provides | Allah |

إنه الله
Verily he is Allah

الله الذي يُنْزِلُ المَطَرَ من السماء

Allah is the one who brings down rain from the clouds

اللهُ الذي يُنْبِتُ الزَّرْعَ والأَشْجارَ

Allah is the one who causes crops and trees to grow

أقول عند نزول المطر: «اللّهُمَّ صَيِّبًا نَافِعًا»

I say when it rains
(O Allah make it beneficial rain)

وبعد نزول المطر أقول:
«مُطِرْنَا بِفَضْلِ اللهِ وَرَحْمتِهِ»

After it rains I say (It has rained with the virtue and mercy of Allah)

الله ينزل المطر من السماء الله الذي ينبت الزرع والأشجار أقول عند نزول المطر: اللهم صيبا نافعا وبعد نزول المطر أقول: مطرنا بفضل الله ورحمته

Allah is the one who brings down rain from the clouds. Allah is the one who causes crops and trees to grow. I say when it rains "O Allah make it beneficial rain". After it rains I say "It has rained with the virtue and mercy of Allah".

الله الذي يُنزِّلُ المطر من السماء

الله الذي يُنبِتُ الزَّرْعَ والأشجار

Allah is the one who brings down rain from the clouds. Allah is the one who causes crops and trees to grow

أُجِيبُ بِالكِتَابَةِ عَلَى الْحُرُوفِ المُنَقَّطَةِ

I trace the letters

من الذي ينبت الزرع والأشجار؟   من الذي ينزل المطر من السماء؟ الله

Who is the one who brings down rain from the sky?   Allah

Who is the one who causes crops and trees to grow?   Allah

أُرَتِّبُ الْكَلِمَاتِ الآتِيَة

I order the following words

الذي	ينزل	المطر	من السماء	الله
الزرع	الذي	ينبت	والأشجار	الله
Is the one	Brings down	Rain	From the sky	Allah
To grow	Is the one	Causes crops	And trees	Allah

16

الله المُنعِم

Allah is the bestower

الله الذي أَنْعَمَ علينا بالسَّمْعِ والبَصَرِ

Allah is the one who blessed us with hearing and seeing

الله الذي أَنْعَمَ علينا بالطعامِ والشَّرابِ

Allah is the one who blessed us with food and drink

أَقُولُ بَعْدَ تَناوُلِ الطعامِ والشَّرابِ:
«الحَمْدُ لله»، وقبله أقول: «بسم الله»

I say after eating and drinking (All praise is for Allah)and before it I say(In the name of Allah)

نِعَمُ اللهِ علينا كَثِيرَةٌ

Allah's blessings are too many

أَشْكُرُ اللهَ على نِعَمِهِ الكثيرة

I thank Allah for all his blessings

اللّه الذي أنعم علينا بالسمع والبصر
اللّه الذي أنعم علينا بالطعام والشراب
نعم اللّه علينا كثيرة .. أشكر اللّه على نعمه
الكثيرة .. أقول بعد تناول الطعام والشراب
الحمد للّه .. وقبله أقول بسم اللّه

Allah is the one who blessed us with hearing and seeing. Allah is the one who blessed us with food and drink. Allah blessings are too many. I thank Allah for all these blessings. I say after eating and drinking All praise is for Allah and before it I say In the name of Allah

اللهُ الذي أنعم علينا بالسمع والبصر – الله الذي أنعم علينا بالطعام
والشراب – نعم الله علينا كثيرة – أشكر الله على نعمه الكثيرة –
أقول بعد تناول الطعام (الحمد لله) وقبله أقول (بسم الله)

Allah is the one who blessed us with hearing and.
seeing. Allah is the one who .blessed us with food
and drink. Allah blessings are too many. I thank
Allah for all these blessings. I say after eating and
drinking All praise is for Allah and before it I say In
the name of Allah

أَصِلُ الْكَلِمَة بِالْمَعْنَى الصَّحِيح
I join the word with the correct meaning

In the name of Allah	Allah is the one who blessed us	بسم الله	اللهُ الذي أَنْعَمَ علينا
With seeing, hearing food & drink	Allah's blessings are many	بالسَّمع والبَصَر والطعام والشَّراب	نِعَمُ الله علينا
Many	I say after eating and drinking All praise is for Allah	كَثِيرَةً	أَقُولُ بَعْدَ تَنَاوُل الطعام والشَّراب
Allah praise is for Allah	Before eating I say In the name of Allah	الحَمْدُ لله	أَقُولُ قبل تَنَاوُل الطعام والشَّراب

أُحِبُّ اللة وأعبدُه
I love Allah and I worship him

أُحِبُّ اللهَ لأنه هُو الذي هَدانِي، خَلَقَنِي، رَزَقَنِي، أَنْعَمَ عَلَيَّ

I love Allah because he guided me, created me, provides for me He has blessed me

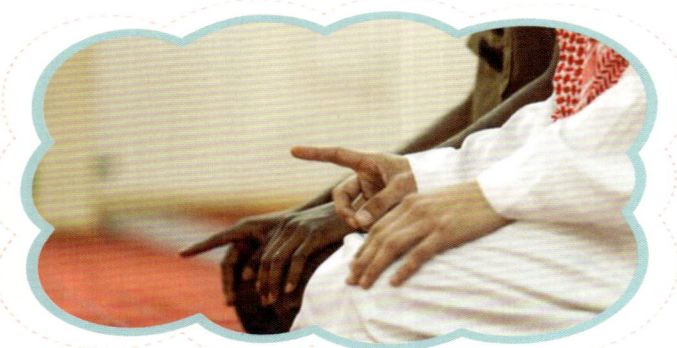

أَعْبُدُ اللهَ وَحْدَهُ

I worship him alone

أَدْعُو اللهَ وَحْدَهُ

I make dua (supplicate) to him alone

أَصَلِّي للهِ وَحْدَهُ

I pray to him alone

خَلَقَنا اللهُ لِعِبادَتِه

Allah created us to worship him alone

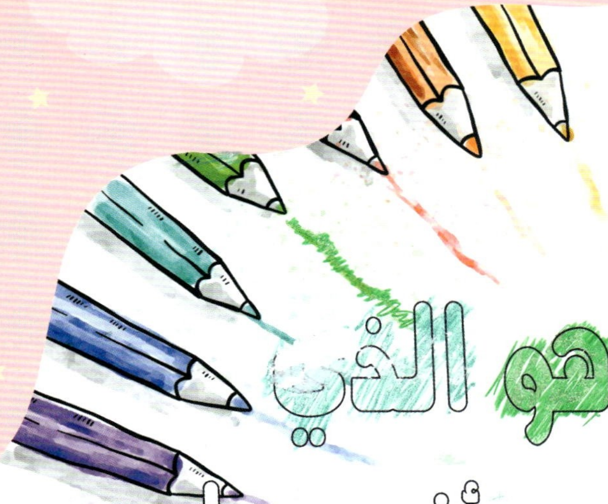

أُحِبُّ اللهَ لِأَنَّهُ هُوَ الَّذِي

خَلَقَنِي وَرَزَقَنِي وَهَدَانِي وَأَنْعَمَ عَلَيَّ

أَعْبُدُ اللهَ وَحْدَهُ - أَدْعُو اللهَ وَحْدَهُ

أُصَلِّي للهِ وَحْدَهُ - خَلَقَنَا اللهُ لِعِبَادَتِهِ وَحْدَهُ

I love Allah because he: guided me, created me, provides for me. He has blessed me

I worship him alone

I make dua (supplicate) to him alone

I pray to him alone

Allah created us to worship him alone

أُحِبُّ اللهَ لِأَنَّهُ هُوَ الَّذِي:

خَلَقَنِي وَرَزَقَنِي وَهَدَانِي وَأَنْعَمَ عَلَيَّ

أَعْبُدُ اللهَ وَحْدَهُ ــ أَدْعُو اللهَ وَحْدَهُ

أُصَلِّي لِلهِ وَحْدَهُ ــ خَلَقَنَا اللهُ لِعِبَادَتِهِ وَحْدَهُ

I love Allah because he: guided me, created me, provides for me. He has blessed me. I worship Allah alone. I make dua (supplicate) to Allah alone. I pray to Allah alone. Allah created us to worship him alone

I worship Allah	guided me, created me, provides for me He has blessed me	هَدَانِي، خَلَقَنِي رَزَقَنِي، أَنْعَمَ عَلَيَّ.	أُحِبُّ اللهَ لِأَنَّهُ هُوَ الذي:
I love Allah because he	Alone	وَحْدَهُ	أَعْبُدُ اللهَ
Allah created us	To worship him alone	لِعِبَادَتِهِ	خَلَقَنَا اللهُ

أُجِيبُ بِالْكِتَابَةِ عَلَى الْحُرُوفِ الْمُنَقَّطَةِ

I trace the letters

مَن أَعبد؟ الله

لِمَن أُصلّي؟ أُصلّي لله وحده

لماذا خلقنا الله؟ خلقنا الله لعبادته وحده

Who do I worship? Allah

Who do I pray to? Allah

Why has Allah created us? To worship him

أَرْكَانُ الإِسْلَامُ
Pillars of Islam

١ـ شَهَادَةُ أَنْ لَا إِلَهَ إِلَّا الله
(مَعْنَاهَا: لَا مَعْبُودَ بِحَقٍّ إِلَّا الله)
وَأَنَّ مُحَمَّدًا رَسُولُ اللهِ
(تصديق خبره، وطاعة أمره، واجتناب نهيه، واتباع شرعه).

To testify there is no diety (god) worthy of worship in truth except Allah. And that Muhammad is the messenger of Allah, Which means we believe him and obey him in everything he has legislated

٢ـ إِقَامُ الصَّلَاةِ.

To establish the prayer

٣ـ إِيتَاءُ الزَّكَاةِ.

Give zakah. (charity)

٤ـ صَوْمُ رَمَضَانَ.

Fast the month of Ramadhan

ه ـ حَجُّ البَيْتِ.

Perform hajj. (pilgrimage)

أَرْكَانُ الْإِسْلَامِ
شَهَادَةُ أَنْ لَا إِلَهَ إِلَّا اللّٰهُ
وَأَنَّ مُحَمَّدًا رَسُولُ اللّٰهِ
إِقَامُ الصَّلَاةِ - إِيتَاءُ الزَّكَاةِ
صَوْمُ رَمَضَانَ - حَجُّ الْبَيْتِ

The pillars of Islam

To testify there is no diety (god) worthy of worship in truth except Allah. And that Muhammad is the messenger of Allah. To establish the prayer, Give zakah, charity, Fast the month of Ramadhan, Perform hajj, pilgrimage.

أَرْكَانُ الإسْلام : شَهَادَةُ أَنْ لا إِلَهَ إِلا الله وَأَنَّ مُحَمَّدا رَسُول الله، إِقَامُ الصَّلاة، إِيتَاءُ الزَّكاة، صَوْمُ رَمَضان، حَجُّ البَيت

The pillars of Islam. To testify there is no deity (god) worthy of worship in truth except Allah. And that Muhammad is the messenger of Allah. To establish the prayer. Give zakah , charity. Fast the month of Ramadhan. Perform Hajj, pilgrimage

أَصِلُ الْكَلِمَة بِالْمَعْنَى الصَّحِيح

I join the correct answer to the appropriate question

حَجّ	صَوْم	إِيتَاء	إِقَام	أَرْكَانُ الإِسْلام	شَهَادَةُ أَنْ لاَ إِلَهَ إِلاَّ الله

الزَّكاة	خَمْسَة	البَيْت	رَمَضان	الصَّلاة	وَأَنَّ مُحَمَّداً رَسُولُ الله

S	Charity	Ramadhan	The house	Prayer	And that Muhammad is the messenger of Allah

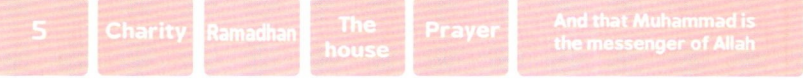

Hajj pilgrimage	Fasting	Giving	establishing	The number of pillars of islam	Testifying there is no deity worthy of worship except Allah

أُرَتِّبُ الْكَلِمَاتِ الْآتِيَة

I place the words in the correct order

صَوْم رَمَضان	إِيتَاء الزَّكاة	إِقَام الصَّلاة	الشَّهادَتان	حَجُّ البَيت

Fasting in Ramdhan	Giving zakah	Establishing the prayer	testimonies	Pilgrimage to the house

أَرْكَانُ الإيمَان
The pillars of Iman (Faith)

١ـ الإيمَانُ بِاللهِ.
Believing in Allah

٢ـ الإيمَانُ بالمَلائِكَة.
Believing in the angels

٣ـ الإيمَانُ بالكُتُب.
Believing in the books

٤ـ الإيمَانُ بالرُّسُل.
Believing in the messengers

٥ـ الإيمَانُ بِاليَوْم الآخِرِ.
Believing in the last day

٦ـ الإيمَانُ بالقَدَر.
Believing in the divine decree

أركان الإيمان

الإيمان بالله - الإيمان بالملائكة

الإيمان بالرسل - الإيمان بالكتب

الإيمان باليوم الآخر - الإيمان بالقدر

The pillars of Iman

Believing in Allah. Believing in the angels . Believing in the books. Believing in the messengers . Believing in the last day. Believing in the divine decree

أَرْكَانُ الإيمَان

الإيمَانُ بِاللهِ – الإيمَانُ بِالمَلائِكة – الإيمَانُ بِالكُتُب –
الإيمَانُ بِالرُّسُل – الإيمَانُ بِاليَوْمِ الآخِر – الإيمَانُ بِالقَدَر

The pillars of Iman

Believing in Allah. Believing in the angels.
Believing in the books. Believing in the
messengers. Believing in the last day. Believing
in the divine decree

أَصِلُ الْكَلِمَة بِالْمَعْنَى الصّحيح

I join the word with the correct meaning

Belief in the divine decree	الإيمَانُ بِاللهِ
Belief in the last day	الإيمَانُ بِالقَدَر
Belief in the angels	الإيمَانُ بِاليَوْمِ الآخِرِ
Belief in the books	الإيمَانُ بِالمَلائِكَة
Belief in Allah	الإيمَانُ بِالكُتُب
Belief in the messengers	الإيمَانُ بِالرُّسُل

MOHAMMED
Peace Be Upon Him

من ذُرية إبراهيم عليه السلام
He is from the lineage of Ibrahim

أَنْزَلَ اللهُ عليه القُرْآنَ الكَرِيمَ
Allah sent down to the prophet The Noble Quran

بشر بنبوته وأمر باتباعه موسى وعيسى عليهما السلام
He was given prophethood, and other messengers are commanded to follow him like Musa and Eisa

أَرْسَلَه اللهُ إلى النَّاسِ جَمِيعًا
Allah sent our prophet Muhammad for all of mankind

يَدْعوهُم إلى عبادة الله وَحْدَهُ
He calls the people to worship Allah alone

مُحَمَّدٌ ﷺ بَشر مَخلوق لكنه أفضل البَشَر، وآخر الأنبياء والرسل
He is a created man, but he is the best of men, and the final messenger

مَنْ أَطَاعَه دخل الجنة
Whoever follows him will enter Jannah (paradise)

أُحِبُّ نَبِيِّ مُحَمَّدًا ﷺ
I love my prophet Muhammad

محمد نبينا

صلى الله عليه وعلى آله وسلم

من ذرية إبراهيم عليه السلام. أنزل الله عليه القرآن الكريم. بشر بنبوته وأمر باتباعه موسى وعيسى عليهما السلام. أرسله الله إلى الناس جميعا. يدعوهم إلى عبادة الله وحده. أفضل البشر، وآخر الأنبياء والرسل. من أطاعه دخل الجنة. أحب نبيي محمدا

He is from the lineage of Ibrahim Allah sent down to the prophet The Noble Quran. He was given prophethood and other messengers are commanded to follow him like Musa and Eisa. Allah sent our prophet Muhammad for all of mankind. He calls the people to worship Allah alone. He is a created man, but he is the best of men, and the final messenger . Whoever follows him will enter Jannah (paradise). I love my prophet Muhammad

نقول عند ذكر النبي : صلى الله عليه وسلم

أحب نبي محمدا. أنزل الله عليه القرآن الكريم

We say when hear the mention of our
prophet: Salla Allahu Alayhi Wa Salam. I love
my prophet Muhammad. Allah sent The
Noble Quran to him

أَصِلُ الْكَلِمَة بالْمَعْنَى الصَّحِيح

I join the word with the correct meaning

My prophet is Muhammad	Musa and Eisa	موسى وعيسى عليهما السلام	نَبِي مُحَمَّدٌ ﷺ
Allah sent to the prophet	Worshipping Allah alone	عبادة الله وَحْدَهُ	أَنْزَلَ اللهُ على نَبِيِّنَا مُحَمَّدٍ ﷺ
He was given prophethood and we're commanded to follow him	To all the people	إلى النَّاسِ جَمِيعًا	بشر بنبوته وأمر بإتباعه
Allah sent our prophet Muhammad	The Noble Quran	القُرْآنَ الكَرِيمَ	أَرْسَلَ اللهُ نَبِيّنَا مُحَمَّدًا ﷺ
Whoever obeys him	From the family of Ibrahim	من ذُرية إبراهيم عليه السلام	مَن أَطَاعَهُ ﷺ
He called all the people to		ﷺ	دعوته ﷺ: يدعو الناس إلى
We say when we hear his name	Enters Jannah (Paradise)	دخل الجنة	نَقُولُ عِنْدَ ذِكْرِ النَّبِي

الطّهَارَة
Purification

بسم الله
Bismillah

أقول قبل دُخُول الحمام: بسم الله
I say before entering the bathroom: Bismillah (In the name of Allah)

غفرانك
Ghufranak

وأقول بعد الخروج: غُفْرَانَكَ
I say after leaving the bathroom: Ghufranak (Allah forgive me)

أُنَظِّفُ مَخْرَجَ الْبَوْلِ والغَائِطِ بِالمَاءِ أو بِمِنْدِيل بيدي اليُسْرَى
I clean my private parts with water or tissue with my left hand

أُنَظِّفُ ثِيَابِي كُلَّمَا اتَّسَخَت
I clean my clothes if they become dirty

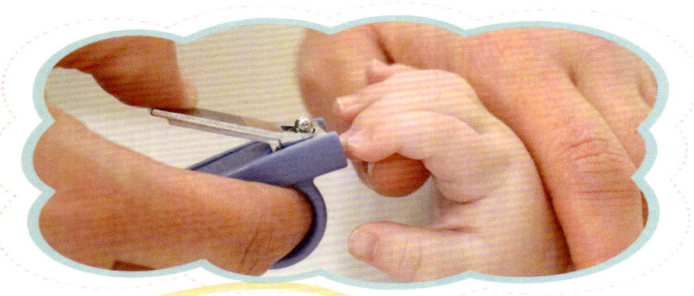

أُقَلِّمُ أَظْفَارِي كُلَّمَا طَالَت
I cut my nails when they become long

أَصِلُ الْكَلِمَةَ بِالْمَعْنَى الصَّحِيحِ
I join the word with the correct meaning

بِالْماءِ أَوْ بِمِنْدِيلٍ بِيَدِي الْيُسْرَى	أُقَلِّمُ أَظْفارِي كُلَّمَا
غُفْرانَكَ	أُنَظِّفُ ثِيابِي كُلَّمَا
طَالَت	أَقُولُ قَبْلَ دُخُولِ الْحَمَّامِ:
اتَّسَخَت	وَأَقُولُ بَعْدَ الْخُرُوجِ:
بِسْمِ اللهِ	أُنَظِّفُ مَخْرَجَ الْبَوْلِ وَالْغائِطِ

I cut my nails when they	With water or a tissue with my left hand
I clean my clothes when	Ghufranak
I say before entering the bathroom	Become long
I say after leaving the bathroom	They become dirty
I clean my private parts	Bismillah

35

صفة الوُضُوء
Description of Wudhu (Ablution)

أَقُولُ: بسم الله

I say Bismillah (In the name of Allah)

أَغْسِلُ كَفَّيَّ ثَلاثَ مَرَّاتٍ

I wash my hands 3 times

أَتَمَضْمَضُ وأَسْتَنْشِقُ ثَلاثَ مَرَّاتٍ

I rinse my mouth and nose 3 times

أَغْسِلُ وَجهي ثَلاثَ مَرَّاتٍ

I wash my face 3 times

أَغْسِلُ يَدَيَّ من أَطْرَافِ الأَصَابِع إلى المِرْفَقَيْنِ ثَلاثَ مَرَّاتٍ

I wash my hands from my fingers time until (including) my elbows 3 times

أَمْسَحُ رَأْسِيَ مع أُذُنَيَّ مَرَّةً وَاحدة

I wipe my head and ears 1 And ears once

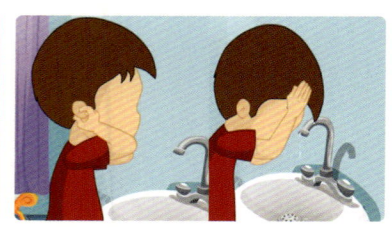

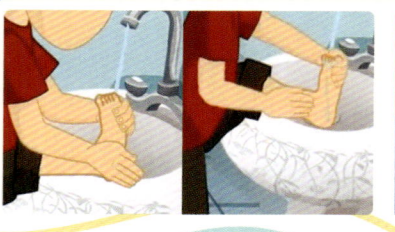

أَغْسِلُ رِجْلَيَّ إلى الكَعْبَيْنِ ثَلاثَ مَرَّاتٍ

I wash my feet until (including) my ankles 3 times

أَصِلُ الْكَلِمَة بِالْمَعْنَى الصَّحِيحِ

I join the correct answer to the appropriate question

أَغْسِلُ رِجْلَيَّ إِلَى الْكَعْبَيْنِ ثَلَاثَ مَرَّاتٍ.	١
أَمْسَحُ رَأْسِيَ مَعَ أُذُنَيَّ مَرَّةً وَاحِدَة.	٢
أَغْسِلُ وَجْهِي ثَلَاثَ مَرَّاتٍ.	٣
أَقُولُ بِسم الله.	٤
أَتَمَضْمَضُ وَأَسْتَنْشِقُ ثَلَاثَ مَرَّاتٍ.	٥
أَغْسِلُ كَفَّيَّ ثَلَاثَ مَرَّاتٍ.	٦
أَغْسِلُ يَدَيَّ مِنْ أَطْرَافِ الأَصَابِعِ إِلَى الْمِرْفَقَيْنِ ثَلَاثَ مَرَّاتٍ.	٧

1	I wash my feet until my ankles 3 times
2	I wipe my head and ears once
3	I wash my face 3 times
4	I say Bismillah
5	I rinse my mouth and nose 3 times
6	I wash my hands 3 times
7	I wash my hands from my fingertips until my elbows 3 times

تَواقِضُ الوُضُوء
Nullifiers of Wudhu

الخارج من السَّبيلَيْنِ (البول ـ الغائط ـ الريح)
**Anything leave the 2 passages
(urine, faeces and wind)**

النَّوْمُ
Sleeping

أَكْلُ لَحْمِ الإِبِلِ
Eating camel meat

أَصِلُ الْكَلِمَةَ بالْمَعْنَى الصَّحِيحِ
I join the word with the correct meaning

Camel meat	**Whatever** leaves the 2 passages	الإبل	الخارج من السبيلين
urine, faeces and wind	**Eating**	البول ـ الغائط الريح	أكل لحم

أُرَتِّبُ الأفْعَالَ التالية
I order the following words

I pray	I perform abution wudhu	I clean myself	أَسْتَنْجي	أتوضأ	أُصلّي

صفة الغُسل — Description of Showering

Make the intention with the heart, say bismillah, then wash the whole body with water, including what is under the nails and hair, with water including rinsing the mouth and nose	أن ينـوي الغسـل بقلبـه، ثمَّ يسـمِّي الله تعـالى، ثمَّ يعمِّم جميع البدن وما تحت الشُّعـور الخفيفـة والكثيفـة بالمـاء، مع المضمضة والاستنشاق.

الصَّلواتُ المَفْروضَة
The 5 daily prayers

من طلوع الفجرالثاني

إلى طلوع الشمس

صَلاةُ الفَجْرِ، رَكْعَتَانِ
Fajr 2 units (Raka'at)

من زوال الشمس — إلى ان يصير ظل كل شيء مثله

صَلاةُ الظُّهرِ، أَرْبَعُ رَكَعَاتٍ
Dhur 4 units

من خروج وقت الظهر — إلى ان يصير ظل كل شيء طوله مرتين

صَلاةُ العَصرِ، أَرْبَعُ رَكَعَاتٍ
Asr 4 units

من غروب الشمس — إلى آن يغيب الشفق الأحمر

صَلاةُ المَغْرِبِ، ثَلاثُ رَكَعَاتٍ
Maghrib 3 units

مغيب الشفق الأحمر

إلى نصف الليل

صَلاةُ العِشَاءِ، أَرْبَعُ رَكَعَاتٍ
Isha 4 units

أَصِلُ الْكَلِمَةَ بِالْمَعْنَى الصَّحِيحِ
I join the word with the correct meaning

The obligatory prayers	Fajr	الفجر	الصلوات المفروضة
I start my day with it	2 units	ركعتان	أبدأ كل يوم بصلاة
Fajr prayer	3 units	ثلاث ركعات	صلاة الفجر
Maghrib Prayer	4 units	أربع ركعات	صلاة المغرب
Dhur, Asr and Isha prayer	5	خمسة	صلاة الظهر والعصر والعشاء

أُرَتِّبُ الْكَلِمَاتِ الْآتِيَةَ
I order the following words

	Dhur: 4 units	صلاةُ الظُّهْرِ، أَرْبَعُ رَكَعَاتٍ
	Asr: 4 units	صلاةُ المَغْرِبِ، ثَلاثُ رَكَعَاتٍ
	Maghrib: 3 units	صلاةُ العَصْرِ، أَرْبَعُ رَكَعَاتٍ
	Fajr: 2 units	صلاةُ العِشَاءِ، أَرْبَعُ رَكَعَاتٍ
	Isha: 4 units	صلاةُ الفَجْرِ، رَكْعَتَانِ

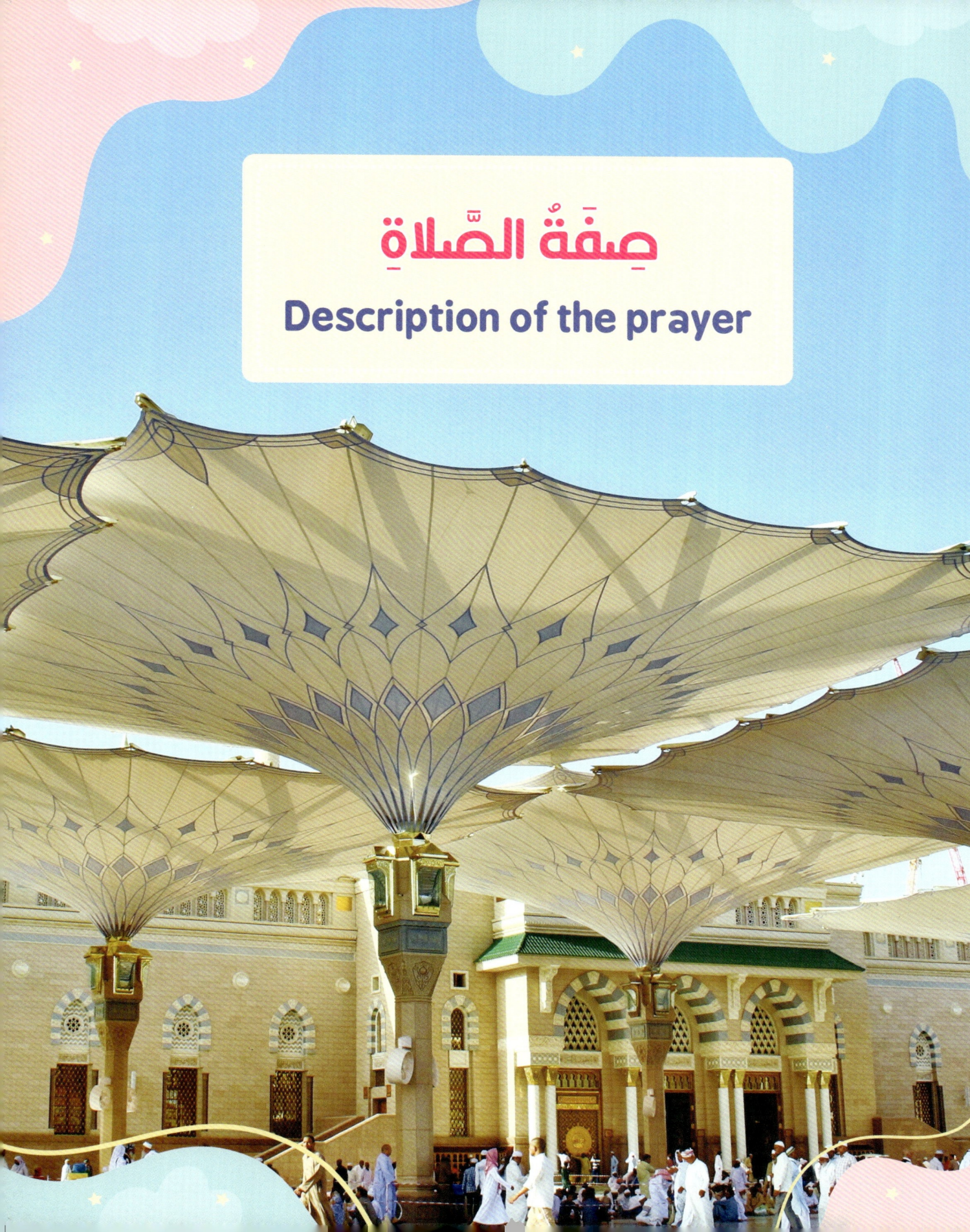

صِفَةُ الصَّلاةِ

Description of the prayer

أَسْتَقْبِلُ القِبْلَةَ قائِمًا

I face the Qiblah while standing

أُكَبِرُ تَكْبِيرَةَ الإِحْرامِ قَائِلًا:
(اللهُ أَكْبَرُ)

I do takbeeratu al-Ihram raise my hands and say Allahu Akbar

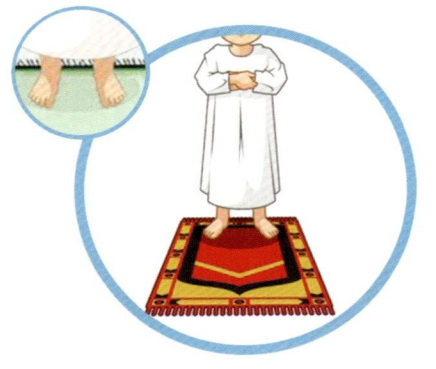

أَضَعُ يَدِي اليُمْنَى على اليُسْرى على صَدْري

I place my right hand over my left on my chest

أَقْرَأُ دُعَاءَ الاسْتِفْتَاحِ: سُبْحَانَكَ اللَّهُمَّ وَبِحَمْدِكَ، وتَبَارَكَ اسْمُكَ، وَتَعَالَى جَدُّكَ، وَلاَ إِلَهَ غَيْرُكَ.

I recite the open dua: Subhanakallahuma Wa Bihamdik, Wa Tabarakasmukah, Wa Ta Aalaa Jaduka, Wa La Ilaha Ghayruk

قْرَأُ الفَاتِحَة: (أَعُوذُ بِاللهِ مِنَ الشَّيْطَانِ الرَّجِيمِ) {بِسْمِ اللهِ الرَّحْمَنِ الرَّحِيمِ (١) الْحَمْدُ للهِ رَبِّ الْعَالَمِينَ (٢) الرَّحْمَنِ الرَّحِيمِ (٣) مَالِكِ يَوْمِ الدِّينِ (٤) إِيَّاكَ نَعْبُدُ وَإِيَّاكَ نَسْتَعِينُ (٥) اهْدِنَا الصِّرَاطَ الْمُسْتَقِيمَ (٦) صِرَاطَ الَّذِينَ أَنْعَمْتَ عَلَيْهِمْ غَيْرِالْمَغْضُوبِ عَلَيْهِمْ وَلَا الضَّالِّينَ (٧)}

ثم أقول: "آمين".. ثم أقْرَأُ مِمَّا أَحْفَظُ من القُرآن.

I recite Surah Al-Fatihah

1. **Authobillahi Min Al-Shaytaanir Rajeem**
2. **Bismillaahir Rahmaanir Raheem**
3. **Alhamdu lillaahi Rabbil 'aalameen**
4. **Ar-Rahmaanir-Raheem**
5. **Maaliki Yawmid-Deen**
6. **Iyyaaka na'budu wa Iyyaaka nasta'een**
7. **Ihdinas-Siraatal-Mustaqeem**
8. **Siraatal-lazeena an'amta 'alaihim ghayril-maghdoobi 'alaihim wa lad-daaalleen**
   - **Then I say Aameen and after that recite what I have memorised from the Quran**

أقُولُ: "اللهُ أَكْبَر"، وأركَعُ، وأَقُولُ: "سُبْحَانَ رَبِّيَ الْعَظِيمِ"

I say "Allahu Akbar" and do Ruku' (bow) and say Subhana Ribyal Al-Adheem

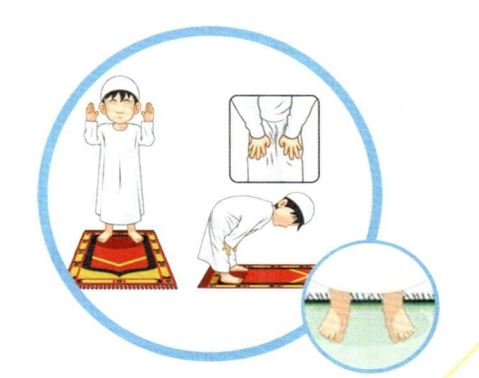

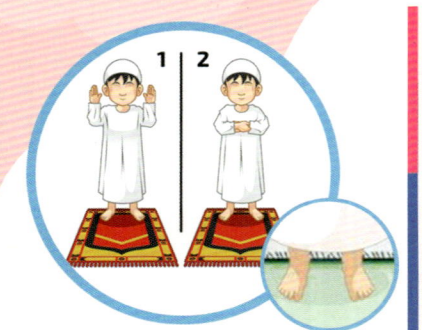

أقولُ حالَ رَفعي من الرُكوعِ: "سَمِعَ اللهُ لِمَن حَمِده".

ثم أقولُ وأنا قائمٌ: "ربَّنا ولك الحمدُ"

I then say whilst on my way to stand up "SamiAllahu Liman Hamidah". Then when fully stood up, I say Rabana Wa Lakal Hamd

أقولُ: "اللهُ أَكْبَرُ"، وَأَسْجدُ، وَأَقُولُ: "سُبْحَانَ رَبِّيَ الْأَعْلَى"

Then I say "Allahu Akbar! And do sujood (prostrate) and say Subhana Rabiyal A'alaa

أَعْتَدِلُ قائلًا: "اللهُ أَكْبَرُ"، وَأَجْلِسِ على قَدَمِي اليُسْرى وَأَنْصِبُ اليُمنى، وَأَقُولُ: "ربِّ اغْفِرْ لي"

Then I get up saying "Allahu Akbar" and sit on my left foot, whilst my right foot is upright and say "Rabighfir Lee" (O My Lord, forgive me)

أقولُ: "اللهُ أَكْبَرُ"، وأَسْجدُ ثَانِيَة، وَأَقُولُ: "سُبْحَانَ رَبِّيَ الْأَعْلَى".

Then I say "Allahu Akbar" and do the second sujood and I say Subhana Rabiyal A'alaa

أَقُومُ للرَكْعَةِ الثَّانِيَةِ قائلًا: "اللهُ أَكْبَرُ"، وَأَفْعَلُ فيها مثْل مَا فَعَلْتُهُ في الركْعَةِ الأولى

I then stand for the second unit of prayer by saying "Allahu Akbar" and then do the same actions I did in the first unit of prayer

أَجْلِسُ بعد الرَّكْعَة الثَّانِيَة لِلتَّشَهُّدِ الأَوَّل، وأَقُولُ: "التَّحِيَّاتُ لله وَالصَّلَوَاتُ وَالطَّيِّبَاتُ، السَّلَامُ عَلَيْكَ أَيُّهَا النَّبِيُّ وَرَحْمَةُ الله وَبَرَكَاتُهُ، السَّلَامُ عَلَيْنَا وَعَلَى عِبَادِ الله الصَّالِحِينَ، أَشْهَدُ أَنْ لَا إِلَهَ إِلَّا الله، وَأَشْهَدُ أَنَّ مُحَمَّدًا عَبْدُهُ وَرَسُولُهُ"

I then sit for the first tashahud and say "Attahiyyaatu lillaahi wassalawaatu , wattayyibaatu , assalaamu 'alayka 'ayyuhan-Nabiyyu wa rahmatullaahi wa barakaatuhu, assalaamu 'alaynaa wa 'alaa 'ibaadillaahis-saaliheen. 'Ash-hadu 'an laa 'ilaaha 'illallaahu wa 'ash-hadu 'anna Muhammadan 'abduhu wa Rasooluhu

إن كانت الصَّلاة ثنائِيَّةً ذات ركعتين أقرأُ الصلاة الإبراهيمِيَّة، ثمَّ أُسَلِّمُ

If the prayer is only 2 units then I say the Ibrahim prayer then say two salams and finish my prayer

وإن كانت الصَّلاة ثلاثِيَّةً أو رباعِيَّةً أقومُ للركعةِ الثالثة، وأَفْعَلُ في بقية صَلاتي مثل ما فعلتُهُ في الركعتين السابِقَتين وأَقْتَصِرُ على قِراءةِ الفاتِحَة

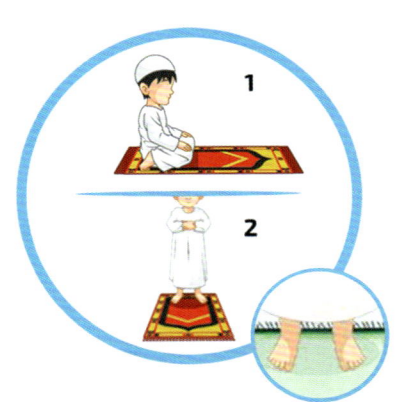

If the prayer is 3 or 4 units, then I stand for the next unit of prayer and do the units of 2 same as I did in the first prayer, except I only recite surah fatihah when standing

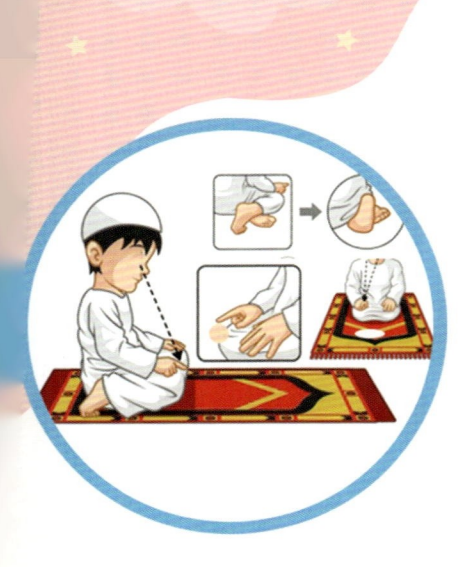

أَجْلِسُ فِي آخِرِ صَلَاتِي وَأَقْرَأُ التَّشَهُّدَ الأَخِيرَ، وَأُصَلِّي عَلَى النَّبِيِّ ﷺ قَائِلًا: "اللَّهُمَّ صَلِّ عَلَى مُحَمَّدٍ وَعَلَى آلِ مُحَمَّدٍ كَمَا صَلَّيْتَ عَلَى آلِ إِبْرَاهِيمَ إِنَّكَ حَمِيدٌ مَجِيدٌ، اللَّهُمَّ بَارِكْ عَلَى مُحَمَّدٍ وَعَلَى آلِ مُحَمَّدٍ كَمَا بَارَكْتَ عَلَى آلِ إِبْرَاهِيمَ إِنَّكَ حَمِيدٌ مَجِيدٌ".

Then I sit for the final tashahud and I send salutations upon the prophet by saying: Allaahumma salli 'alaa Muhammadin wa alaa 'aali Muhammad; kamaa sallayta alaa 'Ibraaheema wa 'alaa 'aali Ibraaheem, 'innaka Hameedum Majeed Allaahumma baarik 'alaa Muhammadin wa 'alaa 'aali Muhammad; kamaa baarakta alaa 'Ibraaheema wa 'alaa 'aali Ibraaheem, 'innaka Hameedum Majeed

أُسَلِّمُ عَنْ يَمِينِي قَائِلًا: "السَّلَامُ عَلَيْكُمْ وَرَحْمَةُ اللهِ"، وَعَنْ يَسَارِي قَائِلًا: "السَّلَامُ عَلَيْكُمْ وَرَحْمَةُ اللهِ".

Then I give salam to my right by saying: As-salamu alaikum wa rahmatullah Then on my left by saying: As-salamu alaikum wa rahmatullah

مُبْطِلَاتُ الصَّلَاةِ
Nullifiers of the prayer

Speaking
Eating or drinking
Laughing
Moving a lot
Breaking Wudhu
(urine, faeces and wind)

الكَلَامُ.
الأَكْلُ أَوِ الشُّرْبُ.
الضَّحِكُ.
الحَرَكَةُ الكَثِيرَةُ.
انْتِقَاضُ الوُضُوءِ (بِبَوْلٍ ـ غَائِطٍ ـ رِيحٍ).

I say in Takbeertaul Ihram	Subhana Rabiyal Adheem	سُبْحَانَ رَبِّيَ الْعَظِيمِ	أقولُ في تَكْبِيرَة الإِحْرام
I say in Ruku (bowing)	Samiallahu Liman Hamidah	سَمِعَ اللهُ لِمَن حَمِدَه	أقولُ في الركوع
I say in sujood (prostrating)	Allahu Akbar	اللهُ أَكْبَر	أقولُ في السجود
I say between the 2 sujood's	Subhana RabiyalA'ala	سُبْحَانَ رَبِّيَ الْأَعْلَى	أقولُ بين السجدتين
I say whilst coming up from Ruku	Rabighfir Lee	رَبِّ اغفِرْ لي	أقولُ في الرفع من الرُّكوع

The opening dua is recited in	Every unit /rak'ah of prayer	كل ركعة	يقول دعاء الاستفتاح في الركعة
Surah Fatihah is recited in	Second unit	الثانية	تقرأ الفاتحة في
The first tashahud is the	Final unit	الأخيرة	التشهد الأول يكون في الركعة
I pray the final tashahud after	First unit	الأولى	أقرأ التشهد الأخير بعد الركعة

Fajr			صلاة الفجر
Dhur	2 Tashahud's	تَشهُّدان	صلاة الظهر
Asr	1 Tashahud	تشهد واحد	صلاة العصر
Maghrib			صلاة المغرب
Isha			صلاة العشاء